THE
MOON

TIM FURNISS

WAYLAND

Spinning through space

THE MOON

Other titles in the series: The Earth ● The Moon ● The Solar System

Find Wayland on the Internet at http://www.wayland.co.uk

All Wayland books encourage children to read and help them improve their literacy.

✓ The contents page, page numbers, headings and index help locate specific pieces of information.

✓ The glossary reinforces alphabetic knowledge and extends vocabulary.

✓ The further information section suggests other books dealing with the same subject.

Cover photographs:
Lunar Prospector in orbit around the Moon, 1998 [main]; astronaut Buzz Aldrin, 1969 [inset left]; *Saturn 5* spacecraft [inset middle]; crescent Moon over California, USA.

Title page: Earthshine on the Moon.

First published in 1999 by Wayland Publishers Limited,
61 Western Road, Hove, East Sussex, BN3 1JD, England

© Copyright 1999 Wayland Publishers Limited

Editor: Carron Brown
Designer: Tim Mayer
Production controller: Carol Titchener
Illustrator: Peter Bull

British Library in Cataloguing Publication Data
Furniss, Tim
  The Moon. – (Spinning through Space)
  1. Moon – Juvenile literature
  2. Moon – Miscellanea – Juvenile literature
  I. Title
  523.3

ISBN 0 7502 2408 8

Printed and bound in Italy by EuroGrafica, Vicenza.

CONTENTS

THE EARTH'S COMPANION

Most nights, we can look up and see the Moon shining bright in the night sky. It always seems to be there. The Moon is our constant companion. We look at the Moon with a sense of wonder, just like the first humans did thousands of years ago.

Apart from the Sun, the Moon is the brightest object in the sky. Throughout each month, the Moon appears to change shape. When full Moon is shining, it looks like a face. We nickname the face 'the Man in the Moon'.

It takes astronauts in a rocket three days to reach the Moon. It would take 9,636 trillion days for a rocket to reach the edge of the known universe.

▼ A full Moon rising over a coastal cliff, Mexico.

A full Moon is so bright that it can cast a shadow.

The Moon orbits our Earth. It is just a small part of the solar system, a big family of nine planets and many moons that orbit our nearest star, the Sun. The Sun is just one of millions of stars in a huge galaxy that we call the Milky Way. There are millions of other galaxies like the Milky Way in the universe. The universe is huge and the Earth, the Moon and the Sun are a tiny part of it.

▼ The nine planets that orbit the Sun.

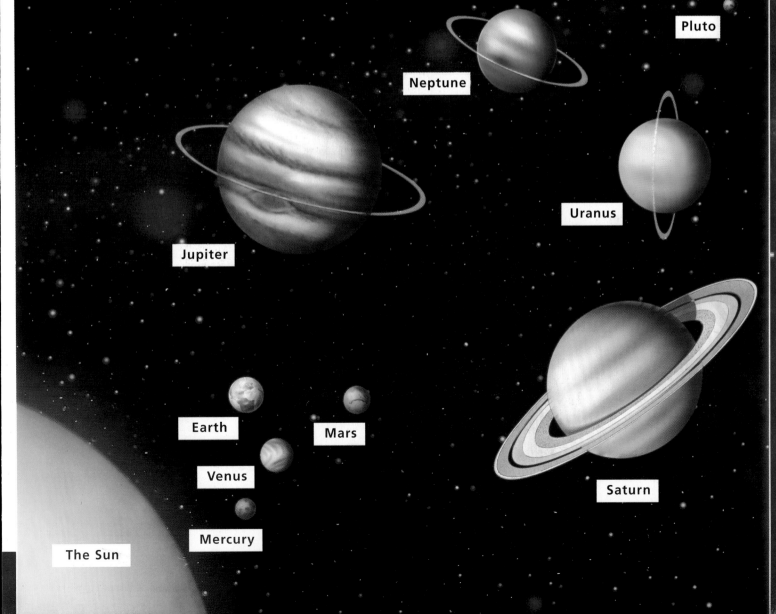

Pluto

Neptune

Uranus

Jupiter

Earth

Mars

Venus

Saturn

Mercury

The Sun

MOONS IN THE SOLAR SYSTEM

Many other planets in our solar system have moons. There are nine planets in the solar system: Mercury and Venus, don't have moons; Earth has one moon; Mars, the red planet, has two; Jupiter, the largest planet, has over 16 moons. Saturn, the ringed planet, has at least 17 moons; Uranus has 15; Neptune has six; and Pluto, the smallest and most distant planet has one moon.

There may be undiscovered moons orbiting these planets which are so small that they have remained unseen by telescopes on Earth.

▼ The Martian moon, Phobos, rises in the west in the Mars sky and sets in the east four-and-a-half hours later.

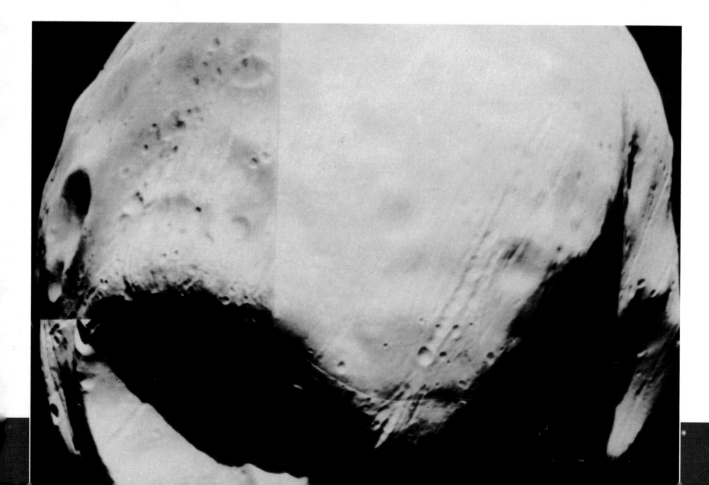

Io, a moon ▶ of Jupiter, has volcanoes that spew sulphur gas 280 km out into space.

Not all moons are spherical like our Moon. Many look like huge rocks. They may once have been planets or rocky asteroids that were captured by the gravity of a main planet when spinning through space. The gravity of the planets may have dragged the 'moons' into orbit around them.

Billions of years ago, our Moon may once have been a planet on its own. It now orbits the Earth.

The bright crescent of the Moon is lit by sunlight, and the dimmer shade is lit by earthshine. ▶

MOON FACTS

The Moon doesn't make any light of its own. The light we see is reflected sunlight. In reality, the Moon has a very dark surface. Only about 7% of the Sun's light is reflected by it. Sometimes, the Moon is also lit up by sunlight reflected off the Earth. This is called earthshine. When earthshine hits the Moon, you will see a bright crescent and a dimmer shade of the rest of the Moon.

The gravity on the Moon is one-sixth that of the Earth. The high jump world record is about 2.5 metres. On the Moon that would be 15 metres!

The Moon is 3,746 km in diameter. It orbits the Earth at a maximum distance of 398,581 km at a speed of 3,680 km per hour. The closest the Moon comes to the Earth is 348,294 km. The Moon takes 28 days, a lunar month, to orbit our planet once.

The Moon only ever shows one side to us because, as it is orbiting our Earth, it is also spinning round. It takes exactly 28 days to make one spin, the same time as it takes to orbit the Earth. We cannot see all the Moon's far side as it is always turned away from us and hidden. The temperature of the Moon varies from 105°C in the bright sunlight to minus 155°C in the shade.

The Moon once orbited the Earth at a closer distance of 64,000 km. It is moving away from Earth in its orbit very slowly.

▼ The Moon is about one-third the size of the Earth, although it looks a lot smaller in this photograph.

THE SURFACE OF THE MOON

When you look at the Moon you can see the famous 'Man in the Moon' face. This is caused by the difference between the light and dark areas on the surface. The lighter areas are covered by craters and mountains. The darker areas, called mares, are large, smooth, flat plains which were mistaken for 'seas' by early astronomers. This explains why they have names such as the Sea of Clouds and the Sea of Tranquillity.

The largest crater on the side of the Moon that we can see is called Clavius, which is 232 km in diameter.

◀ The Moon's surface has many features, such as craters, deep valleys, high ridges, mountains and smooth, dark areas called mares.

The Moon's heated history

The Moon's surface used to be very active early in its history. Meteorites and other rocks crashed down from space on to the Moon, and formed the many craters that we can see on its surface.

When meteorites crashed into the Moon's surface forming craters, the material ejected from the surface formed lines called rays. The rays of the crater Tycho on the Moon's south pole can be seen with the naked eye.

Later, lava oozed out of the Moon's core and through the mantle. It spread across the surface forming the smooth, dark areas we can see, called mares. At the same time, the soft lava was bombarded by more heavy meteorites and other bodies that hit the Moon's surface while spinning through space, creating basins and craters. The Moon's lunar mountains were also formed at about this time by the movement of lava.

◄ The Moon's surface was heated and scarred by the impact of rocks crashing down from space.

Craters great and small

Many large craters were named after famous people, especially famous astronomers. The most spectacular craters are those with 'rays'. Rays are made of material that was ejected from the craters when they were formed by the impact of a meteorite. Copernicus is one of the most famous craters because it is large and very visible. The brightest crater is called Aristarchus. It has very light-coloured dust that reflects light hitting the Moon.

▼ Hadley Rille is a valley that is 135 km long, 370 m deep and 2 km wide. It was visited by the *Apollo 15* astronauts in 1971.

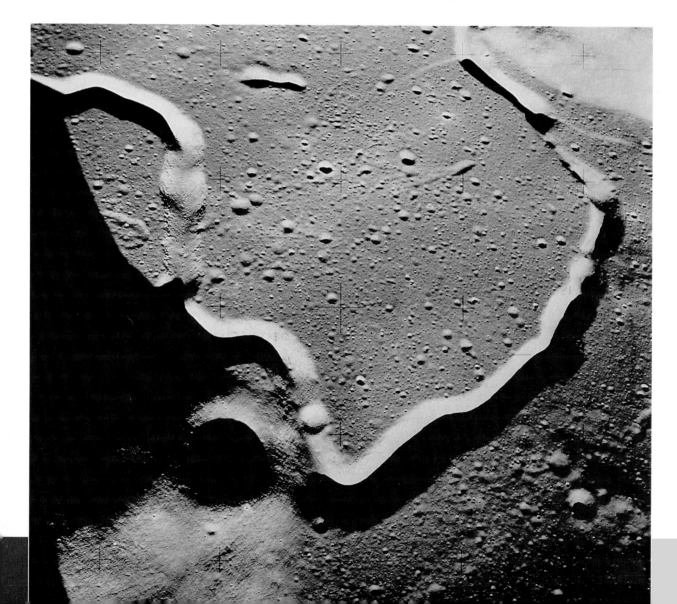

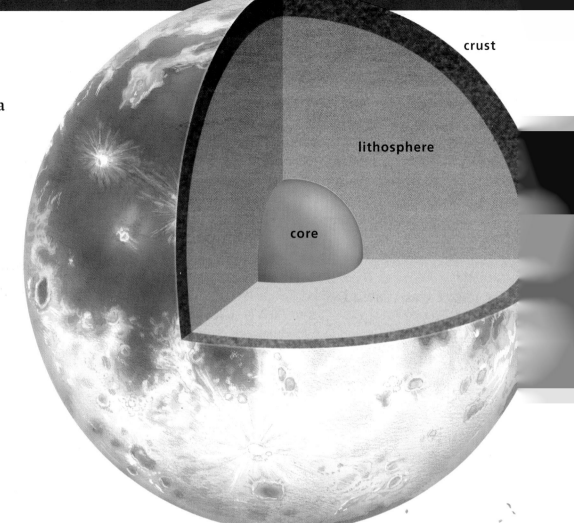

This artwork shows a cross-section of the Moon from its core to outer crust. ▶

crust

lithosphere

core

Under the surface

The Moon is a rocky body made up of several different layers. Its very small central core is about 1,000 km in diameter. This is covered by a layer of lunar mantle, about 600 km thick, called the lithosphere. Finally, there is a 65-km thick layer of outer crust. Spacecraft have detected evidence that there may be water or ice beneath the surface. Ice may be found in very dark, cold areas around the Moon's poles.

The Moon's surface is the same as it was thousands of years ago because there is no atmosphere or wind on the Moon. In 1969, Neil Armstrong, the first astronaut on the Moon, created footprints that will be there for thousands of years.

THE MOON'S MOVEMENT AND EARTH

The effect of the Moon's movement around the Earth causes a reaction on the Earth's surface, in its atmosphere and in the oceans.

If the Earth was one big ocean, the tidal bulge would travel once around the Earth in 24 hours 50 minutes. That is the time of one moonrise to the next.

Tides

The ocean tides are caused by the Moon's gravity. As the Earth turns, the pull of the Moon's gravity causes the water to 'bulge'. On the side of the Earth that's away from the Moon, the effect of the Moon's gravity is less.

▼ A combination of different images made into one photo shows the Earth rising over the Moon's surface.

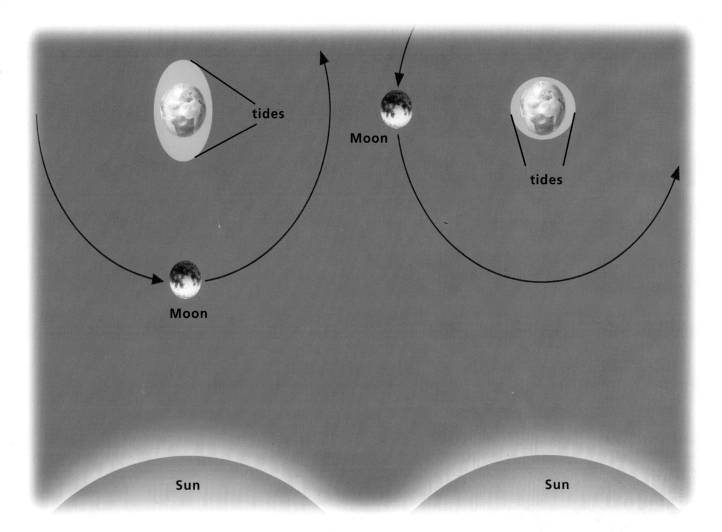

The water lags away from the Earth and forms another slight bulge. In between the bulges, the water is low. It is a bit like a tug-of-war. The bulges are high tides and the low water is the low tide. Sometimes the Sun causes tides as well. When the Moon is in a certain position, it is in line with the Sun and the Earth. The Sun's gravity pull is added to the Moon's making it stronger. This results in very high tides, called spring tides and tides that stay at the same level, called a neap tide.

▲ This artwork shows spring tide (left) and neap tide (right) bulges around the Earth.

The Moon's gravity has slowed the speed of the Earth's rotation. Long ago, it was much faster and days were much shorter.

new Moon

first quarter

full Moon

The Moon rises 50 minutes later each day. This is because the Moon's motion in its orbit is different from the speed of the Earth, so they are always in different positions.

▲ The phases of the Moon go from new Moon to full Moon, then backwards to new Moon again.

Does the Moon change shape?

The Moon appears to change shape during its orbit around the Earth each month. These are called the phases of the Moon. These phases are due to the way we see the Moon as it moves position along its orbit.

A crescent Moon over California, USA. ▶

The invisible Moon

There is one phase of the Moon that we cannot see. This is when the Moon is between the Sun and Earth in the sky. Its far side is lit up instead of the side of the Moon that we can normally see, which is lost in the dark night sky. This is called the new Moon.

Changing times

The Moon orbits the Earth in 28 days. It moves in the same direction that the Earth turns – to the east. The Moon seems to rise and set because it orbits the Earth at a slower speed than the Earth rotates. One day it may rise at 7 p.m. A day later, the Earth will have turned once. The Moon then rises later and the next day, later still. Sometimes, the Moon can be seen during the day. So, the Moon appears in the sky at different times.

▲ The Moon never really changes shape. What we see depends on how much of the sunlit side is turned towards the Earth.

ECLIPSES

As the Moon orbits the Earth and the Earth orbits the Sun, the Earth and Moon sometimes cross over each other's sunlight causing shadows called eclipses. There are two main types of eclipses: solar eclipses and lunar eclipses.

A few hundred years ago, local natives of the West Indies sent food to the ship belonging to the famous explorer, Christopher Columbus, when they were frightened by a lunar eclipse. They thought that Columbus had caused it by anchoring his ship off the island.

Solar eclipses

From the Earth, the Moon seems to be almost the same size as the Sun. The Moon sometimes passes directly in front of the Sun, causing a total solar eclipse. Sometimes, the Moon causes only a partial eclipse when it does not block out all the Sun. There is a third kind of solar eclipse called an annular eclipse. This is when we can see a bright ring around the Moon, caused by seeing part of the Sun when the Moon is a bit smaller in the sky at its furthest distance from Earth.

▼ The Moon blots out all of the Sun's disc causing a total solar eclipse.

During a total lunar eclipse, the Moon turns red due to the colour of the sunsets and sunrises on the Earth reflecting on to its dark surface. ▶

Lunar eclipses

Lunar eclipses happen when the Earth comes between the Sun and the Moon. The Moon orbits the Earth at a slightly tipped angle. This sometimes causes the Moon to pass into the shadow of the Earth. Once in a while, the Moon passes through the shadow fully causing a total eclipse which turns the Moon to a dramatic dark, reddy-brown colour. This light shines from the Earth to the Moon's dark surface. Sometimes, only a part of the Moon enters the shadow, causing a partial eclipse.

The brightness or dimness of the reddy-brown colour of the Moon during an eclipse depends on conditions in the Earth's atmosphere.

MOON EXPLORATION

In the last fifty years, technology has blasted into space. We have learned more about the Moon from spacecraft than we ever did with telescopes on the Earth.

The first spacecraft

The first spacecraft were launched in 1958 but they were not successful. Sometimes the rocket exploded or the spacecraft fell back to Earth. Later, some craft hit the Moon and flew past it, sending back basic science data. Russia's *Luna 2* hit the Moon in January 1959. USA's *Pioneer 4* flew past the Moon in 1959.

The far side of the Moon has remained hidden from humans for thousands of years. No eyes had seen it until the photos from *Luna 3* were transmitted to Earth in October 1959.

▼ This image of most of the far side was taken by *Lunar Orbiter*. The lines are caused by the separate scans the spacecraft made.

The far side of the Moon

In October 1959, most of the far side of the Moon was revealed for the first time. Russia's *Luna 3* flew behind the Moon, took photos and transmitted them back to the Earth. It was a great moment in history. The images from *Luna 3* showed about 70% of the far side and some parts of the Moon that we can see from Earth.

The first people to see the far side with their own eyes were the *Apollo 8* crew. They circled the Moon for the first time in December 1968.

The biggest surprise was that the far side seemed to be almost covered with craters and mountains. There seemed to be no smooth mares.

The far side has many special features, such as the crater Tsiolkovsky and the Orientale Basin.

The Moon's far side from *Apollo 8.* ▶

Further unmanned exploration

In January 1966, Russia's *Luna 9* landed on the Moon and sent back the first images from its surface. It was followed by USA's *Surveyor* spacecraft. *Surveyor 3* scooped up moon dust with a shovel on the end of a robot arm in 1967. *Luna 10* became the first spacecraft to orbit the Moon in 1966. USA's *Lunar Orbiters* mapped the Moon's surface in 1966–7. They sent back spectacular images of almost the whole of the Moon's surface.

The US *Lunar Prospector* spacecraft may have found water or ice under the soil of the Moon's poles. *Lunar Prospector* was launched in January 1998. ▶

An *Apollo 16* astronaut, Charlie Duke, worked on the Moon's surface with the help of the *Lunar Rover.* ▶

The Apollo moon-walkers

Among the most exciting events in the history of the twentieth century were the explorations of the Moon by the first humans in 1969–72. They were called the *Apollo* moonwalkers. There were six landings on the Moon and twelve people walked on it in various areas, from the smooth Sea of Tranquillity to the highlands of Taurus Littrow.

Pieces of *Surveyor 3*, which soft landed on the Moon in 1967, were brought back to Earth by the *Apollo 12* astronauts in 1969.

The Moon landings allowed scientists on Earth to find out more about the Moon's surface. The moonwalkers brought back Moon rocks for them to analyse, and many scientific tools were left on the surface to send information back to Earth.

▲ Buzz Aldrin stands in the lunar dust in this photo taken by Neil Armstrong.

On 20 July 1969, *Apollo 11* made the first manned landing. The Americans, Neil Armstrong and Buzz Aldrin, were the first men on the Moon. *Apollo 12*'s Pete Conrad and Al Bean followed in November 1969. *Apollo 13* did not make a landing. *Apollo 14* landed in February 1971. The moon-walkers were Alan Shepard and Edgar Mitchell. A Lunar Roving Vehicle was driven across the Moon's surface by *Apollo 15* astronauts David Scott and Jim Irwin in July 1971. *Apollo 16* landed in April 1972 with John Young and Charlie Duke aboard.

The last men on the Moon were Gene Cernan and Jack Schmitt in December 1972. No humans have been to the Moon since then.

The six *Apollo* crews came back to Earth with a total of 385 kg of the Moon, which is the same weight as 385 bags of sugar!

The rush to the Moon

The flight of *Apollo 11* was the very first time that humans had left their home planet and landed on another world. It was a truly historic moment in our history. Once achieved, the Moon landings did not seem so important. *Apollo* was an expensive rush to the Moon and when the money ran out, the programme ended. Probably the greatest spin-off from *Apollo* was the view of the tiny Earth as seen from space. Suddenly, the world seemed a lot smaller and lost in the vast universe.

Neil Armstrong's first words when he stepped on the Moon were, 'that's one small step for man, one giant leap for mankind'. He did not say 'a man'!

▼ Geologist astronaut Jack Schmitt of *Apollo 17* took samples of the Moon's surface to examine.

OBSERVING THE MOON

It is easy to observe the Moon. By just using your eyes, you can make out the mare or 'sea' areas. You can even see some of the bright features, such as the rays coming from the crater Tycho during a full Moon.

Through a pair of binoculars, the scene is transformed to a fantastic sight. You can see many craters and even the mountains. They are best seen during the phases of the Moon rather than the full Moon.

Larger telescopes have motors on them so that they can match the Moon's speed and follow it as it moves across the sky.

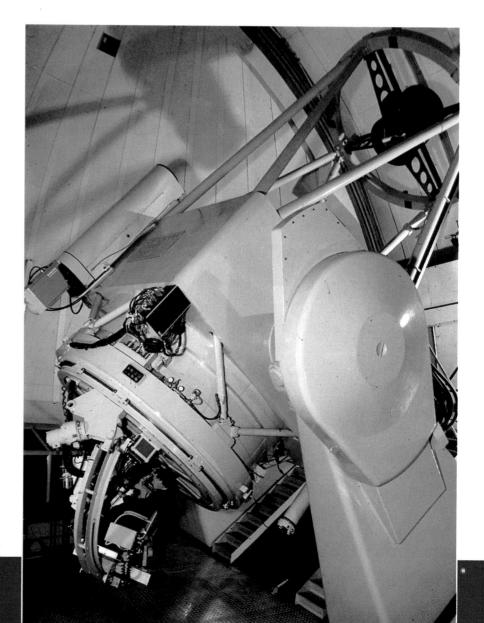

Powerful telescopes with motors such as this one are kept in observatories. ▶

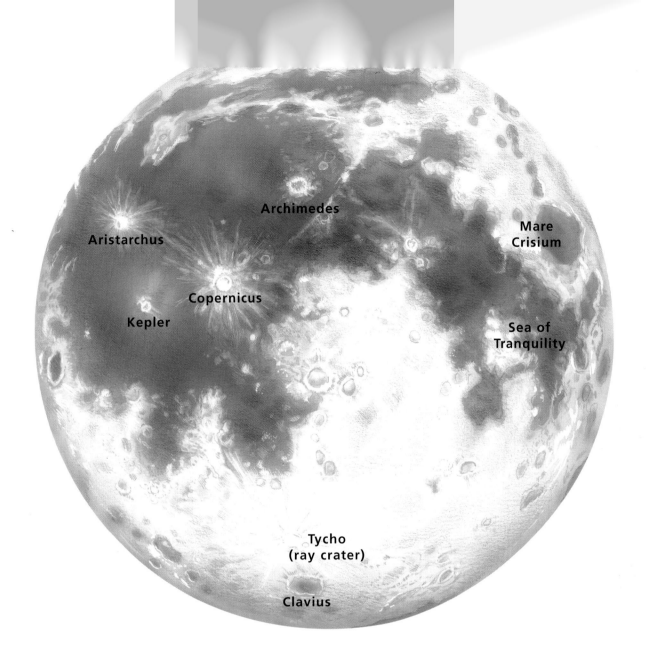

Aristarchus

Archimedes

Mare
Crisium

Copernicus

Kepler

Sea of
Tranquility

Tycho
(ray crater)

Clavius

A small telescope can show even greater detail. If you hold the telescope in your hands, it might be difficult to keep it still. So place the telescope on a stand or a tripod to help you. However, the Moon never stays still and its movement across the sky can seem to be faster when looking through a telescope. So the telescope has to be moved slightly sideways to keep up.

▲ A map of the Moon. The Mare Crisium, top right, is the Man in the Moon's left ear.

The first map of the Moon to be drawn using observations through a telescope was made in July 1609 by Thomas Harriot of England.

TOPIC WEB

THE MOON

MATHS

Measurement: e.g., diameter, distance in orbit.

Compare the sizes of the Moon to the Earth and the Sun.

Describe the different shapes of the Moon.

ART AND CRAFT

History of art: look at how the Moon has been drawn and painted through history in different parts of the world.

Draw or paint a picture of the Moon, drawing in the mares and craters.

DESIGN AND TECHNOLOGY

Look at the design of different spacecraft and explain why they are those shapes. Design your own spacecraft.

MUSIC

Compose a piece of music that begins with the take-off of a spacecraft through to landing on the Moon's surface and exploring.

HISTORY

Find out about what people thought about the Moon in the past: e.g., through myths and legends.

ENGLISH

Imagine that you had travelled to the Moon with one of the space explorers. Write a 'newspaper article' about what you saw and did on the Moon's surface.

SCIENCE

Forces and Movement: gravity

Light and dark: e.g., where does the light on the Moon come from; the changing phases of the Moon; eclipses.

GEOGRAPHY

Landscape features: e.g., what are the main differences between Earth and the Moon and why.

Weather: think about why the Moon has no weather and how this affects the Moon's surface.

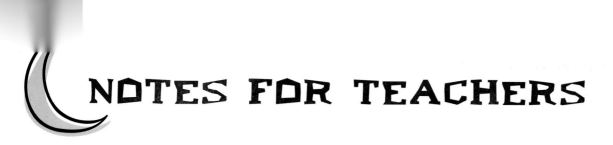

NOTES FOR TEACHERS

Chapter 1 – The Earth's companion

Ask pupils to make a diary of the time and days they see the Moon, what time it rose or set, what was the phase. Ask them to draw the phases as they see them.

Chapter 2 – Moons in the solar system

Demonstrate the movement of the Earth and the Moon as they orbit the Sun. Stand a pupil, the 'Sun', in the middle of a large room. Get two people to stand some way away. Let one walk slowly round the 'Sun' in a circle anticlockwise, the 'Earth'. The other should walk around the 'Earth' while at the same time walking round the 'Sun'. If the 'Moon' walks in a spiral movement, while the 'Earth' moves slowly within the spiral and it is done slowly enough, it should not be too difficult.

Chapter 3 – Moon facts

Put a ball on the end of string and whirl the string around the simulate an 'orbit' and how the speed keeps the 'ball' at the end of the string.

Chapter 4 – The surface of the Moon

Show how craters are made by making a 'mud pie' mixture on the tray and dropping stones on to it.

Chapter 5 – The Moon's movement and Earth

• Explain gravity as the force of two objects against each other.

• Demonstrate how the phases work by using a torch (sunlight) and a large ball (the Moon) in a dark room. Place the ball in front of the pupils and then ask one pupil to move the torch around the room shining at the ball while the others stay in the same place watching the ball. They will see the Moon go from a full Moon when the sunlight is in front of the Moon to a crescent shape when the sunlight is just behind the Moon.

Chapter 6 – Eclipses

Demonstrate how an object eclipses another by moving across it, using a light and a ball, and show how you can create the effect of a lunar eclipse using a light and two balls.

Chapter 7 – Moon exploration

Find extracts of newspapers from 1969 and imagine the excitement of exploring the Moon. Ask the pupils to write a magazine article as if they were the first person to explore the Moon.

Chapter 8 – Observing the Moon

One evening, observe the Moon. Spot the 'seas' and name them. See if you can pick out Tycho and a few other of the brighter craters. Use a pair of binoculars to observe closer. Use the map on page 27 as a guide.

 GLOSSARY

Asteroids Small rocks that orbit planets.

Astronauts A person who travels through space in a spacecraft.

Astronomers People who study the stars.

Atmosphere The air around the Earth.

Basins A wide, rounded dip in a surface.

Core The central part of something.

Craters Deep, wide holes on a surface.

Crescent A narrow curve; the Moon is crescent-shaped in two of its phases.

Diameter The length drawn between one side of a circle or sphere to the opposite side through its centre.

Galaxy A group of stars in the sky.

Gravity A pulling force that brings objects closer to a large object, such as a planet.

Lava Melted rock that has surfaced from the core of a planet.

Lunar Having something to do with the Moon.

Mantle The inner layer of a moon or planet that lies between the core and the surface.

Meteorites Rocks that float through space, occasionally drawn by gravity to the surface of a large object such as a planet.

Optical illusion When you see something which is really something different.

Orbits To go round.

Phases Stages of change, i.e. the different shapes of the Moon that we can see from Earth.

Solar system The Sun and the nine planets that orbit it, and their moons.

Spherical Round all over, like a ball.

☾ FURTHER INFORMATION

Web sites:
www.fourmilab.ch/earthview/vplanet.html
You can view the Moon from this website and find out up-to-date information on the different phases among other facts.

spaceboy.nasda.go.jp/note/Tansa/E/Tan_e.html
This site contains information on Moon exploration by spacecraft, with updates on future exploration and projects.

www.nasa.gov/   This is NASA's homepage which contains pictures and information about ongoing space exploration.

Books:
Neil Armstrong (Heinemann Profiles series) by Sean Connolly (Heinemann, 1998)

I didn't know that you can jump higher on the Moon by Kate Petty (Watts, 1997)

The Gobsmacking Galaxy by Kjartan Poskitt (Scholastic, 1997)

The Kingfisher Book of Space by Martin Redfern (Kingfisher, 1998)

The Science of Gravity by John Stringer (Wayland, 1999)

Sun and Moon by Patrick Moore (Riverswift, 1996)

Places to visit:
The Science Museum, Exhibition Road, South Kensington, London (Tel: 0171 938 8000) has many exhibits about rockets, satellites and other spacecraft, some of which have orbited the Moon.

The Planetarium, Euston Road, London (Tel: 0171 935 6861) has programmes about planets, space and the stars, and how they are explored by spacecraft and satellites.

Picture acknowledgements:
The publishers would like to thank the following for allowing us to reproduce their pictures in this book: Bruce Coleman Ltd./Dr Scott Nielsen 17; Eye Ubiquitous/NASA 2, 10, 18, 25; Genesis Photo Library *cover*, 6, 7, 9, 12, 20, 21, 22, /NASA *cover*, 12, 23; Science Photo Library 11, /David Nanuk 2, 4, /Royal Greenwich Observatory 26, /John Sanford *title page*, 8, /Frank Zullo *cover*, 3, 16, 19; The Stock Market/NASA 14.

The illustrations on pages 5, 13, 15, 16 and 27 are by Peter Bull.

INDEX

All numbers in **bold** refer to pictures as well as text.